Mark Andrew Bogdania

Jump Joint

&

Other Scribbles

Fall 2009

OTHER TITLES BY
MARK ANDREW BOGDANIA

The Amazing Double-Life of Marcus Pivo:
Lviving with Agent Orange

Australia
Haiku'd Adventures in Oz

Spilt Apples
Knotted Shoutouts from Marge's Pet Shop

Mark Andrew Bogdania

Jump Joint

&

Other Scribbles

Published by BogDania Productions

www.markbogdania@live.com

ISBN: 978-0-615-32579-8

ISBN 978-0-615-32579-8

9 780615 325798
90000

I peered into the window

to see what I could see;
So little did I know
of what made me, me.

Prologue

Asking an aspiring poet his influences is like asking Ernest Hemingway his thoughts on bullfighting. You'd probably receive a myriad of answers depending on the time of day, macro-weather patterns, or level of sobriety of the interviewee. Though, if you caught me on a Saturday morning after much caffeine and yoga practice I might be able to provide a few lucid insights into my Weltanschauung, or cognitive philosophy. I'd probably say that John Keats's *Endymion* was divinely inspired and Samuel Beckett's *Whoroscope* was more than mere tribute to "gub'ment cheese." Then I'd add that Carl Sandburg's work gave everyman a voice when he really needed it and that Eugene Field provided lyrical magic to even the most pedestrian of life chores.

The sage boat makers of New England will tell you that a "jump joint" is the flush joining of planks on a carvel built wooden vessel in which the edges are laid close and caulked to make a smooth finish. This is, as compared with a clinker built vessel whose hull contains over lapping planks such as those employed by the intrepid, early Viking sea-goers.

Whether the difference reflects a technological advancement or merely an improvement in aesthetics has been strictly a matter open for debate

amongst generations of maritime craftsmen and surely cannot be further defined here. For my purposes a *Jump Joint* is a starting point for my imagination as it leaps from Hamlet to Romeo, Satchel Paige to Roy Bean, Nefertiti to Venus, and Romulus to Oppenheimer. It is my fervent wish that the reader's journey through these waters be as uplifting as the waves of the North Atlantic on a cool spring morning and that any heavy-lifting, or portage be done on my shoulders.

As I add more Freudian fodder to the fireplace this is probably an opportune moment to provide my favorite joke which is probably older than the *Book of Thoth* and must have given the Emperor Claudius some needed comic relief. It goes, "two guys are walking in the forest when they come upon a bear and one guy sits down and starts to put on his running shoes while the other guy looks at him incredulously and tells him that can't outrun a bear. The fella finishes tying his knots and replies that he doesn't have to outrun a bear."

In the following pages of this humble tome I hope to better define the crowded intersections of what I've seen, heard, felt, learned and breathed in through my first forty-six and half years of walking upright on this planet.   These works range from an ode to a child frozen in time in *The Audience* to lessons learned in atomic bomb-making, *Prometheus 'Splained.* You can glimpse some family history in *Bean Pole Jones, Jenerations* and *Stockyard Blues,* read tributes to my Mom and Dad in *The Gentle Woman from Crawford County,* and *Touch 'em All,* discover some my insecurities in *Pod Life* and *Tennis Court Oaf,* travel with me in *Space Junk, She Speaks Thunder* and *Aeolian Dreams,* and possibly learn of some personal erogenous zones in *Anatomy, Gravy* and *My Jones.* In the end these are after all just words on a page, but they are my words, reflecting the beauty and the pain I've witnessed and giving some voice to hoping that I never stop dreaming and to dreaming that I never stop hoping.

Mark Andrew Bogdania

October 13, 2009

Contents

Haiku's & Sonnets

Parting Thoughts

Jump Joint

Jump Joint

Boxes, boxes…
What's in store?
Quote dat raven…
Never more.

Ever, ever…
Did I see.
Such vixen as…
Annabel Lee.

Priest, priest…
What's your fratres?
Leap de threshold…
Marmar matters.

Jumping, jumping…
Grabbin' some air.
Spiking da punch…
Over there.

Triumph, triumph…
Seize da crown.
Play it up…
Marble town!

Oh yeah, Ooh yay…
Ready to bounce.
Rolling dem bones…
Yo Pounce!

Harper, harper…
What's your gift?
Eat, drink, live…
Lyrical riff.

Street sign, stop sign…
What it say?
The pavement's hot…
Steps play.

Walking, walking…
Showing de way.
Red rabbit ran…
Hops today.

Amun, amen…
How to pray?
Feed your spirit…
Soulful clay.

Molding, moulding…
To what form?
De function defines…
Worldly norm.

Bebop, bebop…
What's de frequency?
Tune it in…
Street diplomacy.

Talking, talking…
Ever de defender.
Word it up…
Ice-cream vendor.

Other Poems

Phisher Kings o' Clarendon Park

Dreamin' under de Cott'nwood
groom'd tall grass 'n splendor,
preenin' our spangled spans
'n lure o' practice'd candor.

Munchin' catkins on the green
toasting aments w'in costume'd opera,
rube to foster diamond leaf
'n league of Linnaeus Lepidoptera.

Emtomb'd in jazz chrysalis
suspended state 'n pupation,
caterwaulin'de larvae'd coda
united w'in divided nation.

Shepherds o' de verdant lot
knott'd men o' furrowed bark
wollerin' 'bout wicky wacky woo.
clothe'd to hide yon jaded lark.

Holdin' court 'n curried clover,
keepers o' kno'ledge keen
viziers to Cahokian Pharoahs,
sent to walk a boundary mean.

Debatin' de strengths o' Scudder's Treatise
serve 'nd volley o' reason'd premise
fishbonin' de seeds o' progress
written 'n de stars o' promise.

Wailin' under de milky'd way
'til dust emerge'd from slak'd throat;
cup drain'd dry, omen indeed
quest to run 'n hide bullboat.

Good times pre'empted 'pon winds o' rage
all were tried w'in de tempest
skeeter 'n Buck whisk'd away
still we grasp'd Cabrini's breast.

Sippin' ginger beer 'n torn tornado
Satchel 'nd Ted jus' playin' catch
Arthur's smoke wafts 'long de Ave
worth the price of twice-bill'd match.

Jackie donned de regal threads
'nd led us bums across de line
black cat as badge o' honor
how sweet de grape, how sweet de wine.

Dynamitin' fireflies 'n dust'd dusk
rouge pirogues set adrift
serpentinin' thru ribbons o' rivers
mine o' sorrow'd loss to sift.

Sprawl'd upon de frigid steppe
treasure'd cache 'n hollow'd stump
waintin' 'pon de promised melt
givin' chase to Camelot'd hump.

Pushin' pieces on chessboard checker
two over, one up, 'o one up, two over
funny how de knight moves
hoppin' de bars 'monst de plover.

Our Queen, a rappin' star o' misery
steely'd squaw hood ornament,
Nefertiti o' Monster Point
Madonna from de heavens sent.

A tourney rais'd 'mongst de ballers
sure to be no compromise
for twas 54-40 by half
so over said we to de wise.

Then word spread out about de street
Bishop went 'nd brais'd de beef
He'd gone 'nd pawned de axe
givin' de gas to brisket thief.

The run was on to castle keep
de lakeside lads rain'd down de threes
Cleveland went 'nd check'd de lane
spinnin' de majic 'n de breeze.

Populus deltoides let loose de spour
detrital haircuts o' spring lament
startin' up de cycle anew
spectacle'd bridge o'er trouble'd torment.

Monarch's o' de mara meadow
wanderers 'n de milkweed land
hewin' kayaks out o' shitake clouds,
waltzin' 'tildas 'n de sand.

Shootin' waves to Devil's Head
fishin' for whales 'pon de beach
taxin' de salt 'n salute to peace
Ghandi's all 'n civic breech.

Stretchin' out 'monst de rushes
joy 'pon reaching' stage imago
ring'd brand on jaywalker
ridin' high 'n Oz raid echo.

JB, Cutties, forty ouncers
we dreamt o' better things,
doublin' down to naturals
a club in flight 'pon papilion wings.

Stockyard Blues

Armchair Freuds ravage well
'round paths where angels daren't dwell
tho tortured dreams cause disdain
in tender souls long purged to hell.

Who could guess who gets the gain?
Where sleazy lawyers vend your pain
for mere glamour shots in magazines.
must one wonder when passions wane?

In lands where fat do feast upon lean
allowing dull shouts to drown the keen
such madness tries the strongest heart
as love is felt tho seldom seen.

Yet you have to play your part
heave the bale and load the cart
so clowns can frown and lions tame
while infernos blaze as drawn through art.

Pious parsons 'll quote the same
enlightening roles in the gilded game
for those who toil for others fame
and blithely ask, "What's in a name?"

Bean Pole Jones

Bean Pole Jones was a weary ole miner
if need be gold then he had a pot.
Thru life o' toil he be no whiner
e'en when coal shaft was all he got.
Til one day the banker stopped in for a chat
"Seems ye be a bit lean on account"
Rotund fob spake as watch fell in lap.
"'Tis true o' the pickens
if they be slim, then who be fat?"
"More industry my lad is my advice;
Bootstrap! Bootstrap!
Fight! Fight! Fight!"

So Bean Pole grabb'd his gunny 'n pick
hummin' a tune on down 'n the hole,
salty as Jobe tho nary a lick
strong 'n the spirit, strong 'n the soul.
Thru all the day the pick axe he'd swing
'nd shovel it up for penance pence,
pullin' for tent show prince to be king.
Til canary fell silent midst tweet cadence,
gas fire ignite, horror show frightening.
"Go forward! Go forward! No end in sight!
Bootstrap! Bootstrap!
Fight! Fight! Fight!"

So Bean Pole lain heavy head down to sleep,
lantern gone out, gunny o' coal for a rest
deep 'n the mine he said not a peep;
dust for a blanket, silk for a vest.
Dreamin' o' tinged lilies
'n bloom 'long the walk
marquees in letters,
Buck's horn all the talk.
Porter to spare, de Lalee on track;
"Jokes on tap, no time bitter bite!
Bootstrap! Bootstrap!
Fight! Fight! Fight!"

When Bean Pole woke up, what did he find?
His gunny was full o' press'd carbon ice;
Diamonds 'n diamonds 'n diamonds, so nice.
The banker he knew was by now mere pauper;
He paid him a call
to 'ave a chat proper.
Assure'd the poor punter, sooth'd his fears
Scear'd as he were to cast such a pall.
"Seems you be lite in the lode 'n much in arrears,
So put back to it my man and with all your might!
Bootstrap! Bootstrap!
Fight! Fight! Fight!"

Touch 'em All

He never played fair golden game;
Never spiked his way to fame;
Gotham hadn't cause to praise his name.
He left the farm a tenderfoot;
Called up for war-time college major.
Pigskin frolic by freckle-faced teenagers
o'er braggin' rights long before big wagers
revelry of train rides rendered mute.

He never charged Teutonic lands;
Never stormed yon Normand sand;
Ernie Pyle could but understand.
Life of a corporal at Fort Sill;
Minor league angst as tempests wage
Sinkin' ships as war was raged
'til Lil Boy blew winds of change;
Okinawa fit peacemaker bill.

He never designed a world tower;
Never built great seat of power;
Prairie-style was mere flower
where house and store are needed.

Tho' tis the mundane that gives reason
to sow the fields and time the season;
Clear eye scannin' far horizon
where potter's fields are deeded.

He never tried to rope the moon;
Never timed the sun at noon;
Timex ticker wind'd much too soon.
A heart meant to bridge titanic rift;
Head too stubborn to agree
where fever coloured pedigree;
An examined life defined the breed
o' one who gave who had the gift.

29 Forever

Online dating's quite a trick
Shoppin' histories with just a click
Checkin' out each well placed face
"Til you tease me and I ask, "Got a pic?"

A smorgasborg of every race
Awaits eager eyes in the hunt for grace
Too tall, too short, too fat, too thin
On to the next with quickened pace.

So much to sort, where to begin?
Opening lines, "So where ya been?"
Too lame, too smart, too right, too wrong
Such tripe would try a Buddhist's zen.

A world of info to be had for a song
Tho don't question of those among
The most viewed few who do quote Jong
And fly in cyberspace forever young.

Pod Life

I AM NOT BIPOLAR!

Tho I love/hate my mirrored self
and my frenemy suggests I have probissues,
my crude sophistication provides blithe awareness
of the factoids of retro-modernism.

I AM NOT BIPOLAR!

As I igwatch my debit/savings accounts grindle
and prurse the demangels of random destiny
manifesting listless mandatory wishes
upon the solitary masses in bounded infinity.

I AM NOT BIPOLAR!

Tho I am quite cozy in my discomfort,
my mind/body ebbingly maintains a wearied ease
that unfettered control openly harbours
and as I pre-plan to be better/worse tomorrow,
I knowingly wonder that in some crazy sense

I AM NOT BIPOLAR!

Prometheus 'splained

How'd you break the bounding chains?
Stony albatross o' woe and pain;
Paperweight 'pon Atomic Age;
Tortured writers, twisted rage.

Was it a mighty hammer stroke?
Or, constant pull of rope?
Tension, tension, ever so taut;
Liver, liver all for naught.

Did the eagle quit the fight?
Or, succumb to Herculean smite?
Hydra's blood in vestigial flight;
Cooled down l'Aquila's bite.

Did the punishment fit crime?
'Twas but spark in ancient time;
That led to flame and civic fire;
Torrid scene o' holy pyre.

Could it be a zero sum game?
God's loss is man's gain?
Control the elements;
Reduce the wonderments.

Might man's folly set earth ablaze?
Bringing 'bout the end of days?
Much revelation in the scripture;
Much the rapture in depicture.

The Little Giant

We thought he was a giant,
tho he only stood five-eight,
A voice to boom a locker room
'nd drive away the hate.

We thought he was a giant,
tho he probably coached the 'skins;
Practiced plays showed the way,
'nd taught us how to win.

We thought he was a giant,
a rocky heart of stone;
Toughest scrap on the map,
'nd baddest to the bone.

We thought he was a giant,
tho you may not know his name;
Boot camp sergeant, right on target,
chalk talk for the game.

We thought he was a giant,
tho he toiled 'n minor leagues;
A record streak not for the meek,
sainted tree for keeps.

We thought he was a giant,
no goal was out of reach;
To a man we'd storm the sands,
'nd take the bloody beach.

We thought he was a giant,
tough love at fast time high;
Mental toughness outranks the roughness,
'nd wings you to the sky.

The Gentle Woman from Crawford County

She came from Crawford County;
Comic child of dust-bowl grit,
nomadic wandering mining stock,
nurtured love of school lamp lit.
Many a hamlet long forgotten trudged;
Hard times prevented life of leisure
as poultry was not found in every pot,
a make-do psyche learned in measure.

She came from Crawford County;
Ginchiest lass of Colgan High,
parochial leanings planted at grass root,
freedom of thought as war waged nigh.
Armistice'd eagerness drove ambition;
To teach hungry boom generation,
bursting bustling schoolhouse seams,
paving the highways of Truman's nation.

She came from Crawford County;
Without a plan for boarders,
her four charges would testify,
you cleaned your plate and followed orders.
Debate was saved for red meat dinners;
Lively as Baptist Sunday sermon siege,
pot roast favored o'er Country Joe's catfish,
gallow'd humor of draft board liege.

She came from Crawford County;
Tho small in stature built,
the temperance of a badger,
from no scrap did she wilt.
Her many clubs and interests;
Could fill a playwright's pen,
tho to truly celebrate her life,
would take a minister's zen.

Haiku's & Sonnets

Lesson Plans

What could a poet teach a warrior?
One who heaves hammer to and fro?
Blunt force with concussive result.
Perhaps the focus of steely resolve?
Sharpening the wit, defining the fault;
That feeds the hearth a molten mix.
The hands that pound the blank to edge;
Smithed in hellfire to ice trilogy;
Sword into plowshare, plowshare into sword.
Fury funneled into lightning strike
rumblin' thunder 'cross prairie'd plain.

What could the warrior teach the poet?
One who weaves the verbal shield?
Platonic twists of angsty grist.
Maybe the power of righteous anger?
Pent up rage, unleashed in tectonic force;
Thrusting downtrodden into the heights.
The hearts that pull the block into place,
Up the Nascan ramparts of fate;
Chasqui to trail, trail to chasqui.
Peace relayed from station to station
conch to herald approaching knight.

How Grey the Hillock

Atlas's shrug changes natur'd season;
Generations toil in Dante's hell
seeking balance in tortur'd reason
as heavy lifting rings ironic bell.

Foundries fountain bullion streams;
Hephaestus fustily tests meager metal
o' those striving for golden dreams
eludin' woes while voidin' nettle.

Caught in assay volcanic hellfire heat;
Cooled in azure waters polar sent
hammer'd to form-fit anvil'd creed
thru glorious Brighid inspired bent.

Praises sung of earth-mounded might;
Hail vernal cup o' elixir'd delight.

Twister

Freight trains roar cross plains,

Chaos, mayhem, all in play;

Pieces reflect lives.

Syndrome

Immune with innocence of youth,
pursuit where prudence spurns,
drunken with daring 'til mute,
hoping before hesitation learned.

Heads wring hands o'er idle prate,
worldly and weary ever the norm,
degraded to dust sanctioned by state,
aversion to appetite true to form.

Orgies of organizations made in haste,
pyramids of power rule rare air,
encore for expectations laid waste,
pride and prejudice exhibited bare.

Allegories of aromas crowd the room,
wanting the whereabouts of wild onion bloom.

Da Hookup

Martyred warrior
Spit the bit of burden
Potato Hill stand.

Summits of Futility

Earth shakes
tho few note.

Injustice steams
lush concrete jungle.

Parasites teem
brisk boundary stream.

Raptor scopes
thru blinded eyes.

Thunder peels
rough onion skin.

Omens bless
a voo-doo curse.

Wrongs added
in long division.

One more never was
to Mount Never Were.

Battle of 2006

Feast to settle things
Wine, kabobs, tomato spread
Paging Doctor Freud.

Mapping

Chief Blackhoof had a brother
he would call no other.
That brother had a daughter
Nanex-se is what they named her.

Brace yourself for what comes next
Paine relievers in the text
Thorpe was tried and passed the test
Jesse Owens outran the rest.

The winding road does tell a song
some ballads take years to right a wrong.
Justice comes in many shapes
When all else fails read the tapes.

Library of Intercourse

Alexandria,
Great Wonder of the world,
dash to Nairobi.

The Traveler

Her sweet tabu was making mud pies;
Hardest grit of deepest ocher;
Telling tales 'n tantric, wryest wit
o' warriors crossing deserts of time
joinin' foreign realms in courtly tact;
Possessin' hearts o' lions, patience o' saints
wieldin' pens and shakin' spears;
Lovely massage o' curried chocolate
mole-baked in midst o' forge;
Eyes of tornadoes in spinning fury
twist'd pieces in roads long trod.

Passion

Musky scents incense,
screaming banshees, torn bed sheets;
The salty aftertaste.

Anatomy

Eyes; hot, seething magma,
molten, tho fluid as Vesuvian streams,
hint more than a well-read novella,
o' wants, needs and dreams to be dreamed;

Hands; steady as Dover 'scarp'd chalk,
betray a quickened pulse in loud exclamation
of quietudes spent 'long rain-fill'd walks,
visioning forays to exotic destination;

Legs; astride with purpose and in tune,
rhythmic in pace, spanning great divide,
twixt time and space on long foretold rune,
Skild warrior's passioned fiery pride;

Lips; liquid licorice to melt hoary ice
from too cold heart yearning to roll Eros dice.

September

Hot, sticky, sweet…
September.

Morning dews of August;
distant memories…
September.

Peeling soft denim;
fumbling with hooks…
September.

Strumming the cello;
chord by chord…
September.

Slithering thru trellises;
winding up alleys…
September.

Rising in tempo;
faster in beat…
September.

Frenetic in pace;
up to crescendo…
September.

My Jones

The nape of the neck.

I plead release
from slavish bondage
to damned unholy fetish;

The nape of the neck.
It barely registers
as valid sportin' prey
yet my passions race to;

The nape of the neck.
Fresh brushed tresses
reveal magnetic object
of my untoward affections;

The nape of the neck.
It shouldn't give such voice
to siren errant kisses 'pon
supple unheralded ground;

The nape of the neck.
The pull draws too strong
I surrender as all is lost.
Longingly I book passage to;

The nape of the neck.
The nape of the neck.
The nape of the neck.

Allure

Wild-flowered meadows hide need
scant breezes windmills shutter.
Skinny calves bawl and bleat
cream is churned to butter.

Her smile concedes certain sadness
that pines as Jane for Edward
with weary wiles for Bertha's madness
as love delayed earns as reward.

Azure eyes mock the sea
amber-spun tresses wave as wheat
ripened on a sun-drenched lea
paired to lips pure passioned heat.

Aura stirs Canute's charge of rampart
as a magnet draws to a steely heart

Gravy

The alarm rings as we untangle.

Grind coffee, chase pearly cay.
Greet morn from odd angle,
must love's scent wash away?

Clad torsos per each role
destined for the patterned play.
Monies multiply, souls winnow
Faustian bargains line the way.

Heads wag tongues,
fashion absolves.

Chaos curries union,
woes dissolve.

The alarm rings tho' we entangle.

Easy View

Speedy racecar clue,
You have to know your limits,
dancing the tango.

Ice

Are you there?

Voice timorously tremblez
to snapping stony silence
in staccato'd rose-pipe bursts.

Manic monkeyz howl
in cellularized space
shardz of truth
betray weary wordz.

The run for morning paperz
promised endocrinic rapture
yet ceded certain crash.

Now she callz in hazy waste,
the wordz drifting along
tweek'd towerz of
panicked paranoia.

Rehab vowz void
as monkeyz claw the door.

Space Junk

Images blur, imagination fades.
What to do? Where to go?
Next city?
County? State?
Continent, planet, solar system?
Hurry! Hurry! Hurry! Hurry! Hurry!
Someone else'll get there first!
Flights increase.
Billions run into trillions,
trillions run into quadrillions.
Off into vast, open, terrifying space.
Boats sailing upon oceans of oceans.
Seeds falling as from a ripened pea-pod,
trickling, trickling, trickling, trickling,
into thick, primordial soups of time.
A new universe found in the abyss,
a new solar system plotted,
a new planet seeded,
a place called ...
Earth.

Arc of Eros

A thousand tales did laud the bole
branched in myriad mirror clothe
launched in ursine orbit round static pole
drawn fixedly as flame to moth
stirring savory stew of oracle'd froth
starting hearts of masses beat
stony cold grey gargoyled Goth
to fiery furnace of Helen's heat
forging wings on Mercury's feet.

Taking flight from eagle'd aerie
'long yon jagged precipic'd cascade
to capture gilded fleece from hoary bestiary
curlingly coiled in dogged wait
data mining the depths of explorer's esplanade
course's cue enchantress bow
sowing dragon's teeth with seeds of Ceres
perchance to reap fair golden flake placer-made
shearing sluiced streams pure porphyry lode.

As Moirae weaves becoming thread
lavish luxor prophetic entwined tweed
Penelope unwinds in shrouded dread
pining lost love in saline'd beads
Odysseus trek in mythic deed
did root home in regal apparel
knelt in prayer of kingly creed
to rule empire of steely breed
Zeus and Djoser's riparian realm.

She Speaks Thunder

I only met her once
- and she asked for my shoes.

Tho' I eyed her approach;
resistance was mere frown
to her toothy written name.

High cheek-boned rap star,
nowhere to seek haven from
pierce-toungue'd, nipple ring'd
absolute iron-jawed maven.

I circled the wagons
to shelter my heart.

Too late.

She camouflaged wild onion
and stole roan colt of love.

As cougar chases eagle
steppin' along marred walls
manifested in karma
runnin' thru ribbons of lost falls.

Seven devils bowed wait;
booming voices of
reason-robed fate.

The millions to keep
Train'd in sainted joy.

Now to eternity.

I only met her once
- and she asked for my shoes.

The Edge

A fine exists
'tween now and endless eons
of endless abyss.

Psalm of Mars

If Venus was just mine for night;
Clouds would hold the rain in spite.
Pie-eyed moon would pull the tide;
Rolling dough to baker's side.
Crimson waves would rise in bloom;
Cladding Eve for wedding groom.
Orbits would sync and stars align;
Casting Pollux a Magi sign.
Ears would envy the eyes domain;
Seething beauty of hurricane.
Sounded fury of comet sight;
Clams would hold their pearls so tight.

Scorching sun would quit the fight;
If Venus was just mine for night.

Blackberry Bread

Oony Bissasha
Choctaw manna sweet as wine,
good for what ails ya.

Live Bait

The allure is too strong,
your musk can't be wrong;
Scents mock my ears
as I taste your song.

Festival in bloom,

Spins room to room;

I spy your guise

feeling through womb.

Possessing no fears,
treasure so near;
Hunger traces fate
as lust steams mirror.

Attraction too great,
impulse drives wait;
Booty incites rage
climax upon stage.

Tilt

Angled best of all,
always to have loved the fall,
dulcet Octobers.

7even Year Feast

Did they mock you?
Trivialize your travails?
Couldn't they understand?
Not even if they heard it?
How it hurt when they took the golden stairs;
banish'd you from Xanadu in the heavens,
massacr'd by the millions,
left to roam vast steppe alone.
A man of peace in a land of war.
Was it a river that brought you back?
Or, a dream too stubborn to die?
Walking the land bridges of time and space.
Waiting for good as the soul starved.
And now…
Heart, hands and head sync'd.
The boundaries met,
The table set.
A procession begins….

Sumomora

Bulldog nose guard tough,
fired in Hapon foundry steel
anchor on the loose.

Ode to Horsehide

Red stitching to mirror the globe;
Tectonic traced rift o' ridges,
leather'd patchwork o' brilliant simile.

The feel of a child's cheek;
Smelling of wetland dew,
promising a world anew.

The touch of eternal youth;
To stretch, to stride, to kick, to pitch,
to chase in verdant fields.

Pop flies drift as continents;
To endless summer breach,
a sphere within your reach.

Octobers

Long shadows of Fall
tell a tale known only to the sun.
Warming tilt haunts memory as Summer
cedes to frosty autumnal wilt.

Wave crests crash in crescendo
as storms beckon beach regression.
Promises stowed in lieu of deceits
cold realities glacially approach.

World Series

Can a life be forlorn
chaped by Swedish porn?
Selling soap can get boring
mobs do crave noble gorings.

The Dutch do scheme
in Hong Kong dreams
while czarists tilt
at windmilled spleens.

A power void of great extent
invites you in to pitch a tent.
Circus barkers of every wean
cry and wail to make the scene.

Tho never lampoon Rockerfeller's charity
'tis easier sport to obscure clarity.
As leader's past were trust busters
today's wear blinkers as exo-dusters.

The globe spins faster every turn
stakes are raised, cities burned.
Each and all want to make the news
who is next to pay their dues.

Hometown Heroes

Father Quigley taught
Andy, Opie and the lot,
'n huddled masses.

Jenerations

The mounds we danced upon
rose from our tombs;
Loving bones as building blocks,
Legos in frozen time.

The waters we swam in
Absorbed our life juices;
Stirring pungent potent potable;
Distilled into few drops.

The air we soared through
grew with our breath;
Monsoonal winds of rage:
Reduced to mere gasps.

The fabric of our bounded lives
Woven in blood-stained ink;
Graffiti to the unfamiliar;
Manna to the washed.

Fate

Art conjugates life,
Danger stranger than fiction
Kept 'n fishbowl glass.

Tennis Court Oaf

The return of your volley
results in pure folly.
To bring your backhand to bear
demands tantric rally.

Blistering serves slice through air
inducing net charge as if by dare,
reaching to claim errant chance
and find finish with flair.

There's more to this dance
than pomp and mere circumstance
for the roles we portray
can change in a glance.

Puzzling parameters on grass vs. clay
parts cast and recast as predator and prey,
portends the import of who wins the day
yet pales in contrast to who steels the play.

Family Planning

Mish/Mash, sour hash;
Can u do without a man?
Distrust/mistrust;
Why the fuss?

Will/Nill, strong pill;
Where are u without a gal?
Deconstruct/reconstruct;
What the f*ck?

Chunky Lovin'

Rounded hips bear chase
Clay biscuit in a bastet
Throwin' stick fer peace.

The Manger

How could Josef know?
A virgin with child,
and he a laughingstock?
The donkey brayed,
as the Magi prayed.
If he be a fool,
then who be king?
The occurrence so timely
From Alexandria to Roma.
Or, was it in Bethlehem?
At a crowded inn in a barren land?
Who coughed in the crib?
What was heard in the night?
Above the fray and fracas
watching child crawl in hay.
Josef knew and he knows
thru august crease of Eve.
Eons of shepherding flocks
Midst fields of semolina,
Stepping 'long paths cut into prairie
To fortunate lake of promise.
Was it a dream?
Or, merely a manger scene?
How could Josef know?

The Audience

What if
you wrote a song
to the not yet born?

Would it
have the impact
of one hand clapping?

Could they
hear muffled, mendelic melodies
of accordion symphonies?

Would they
sense innate correlations
in spiritual echoes?

Or, might they
rage 'gainst the welded mask
of obscene obscurity?

Forever frozen
into
wombs of possibility.

Wake Young Warrior

Wake young warrior greet the morning light,
Beastly howls of night wane to dry complaint;
Rise, rise: Carpe Diem yours by right.

Drunkards slur, stagger, infer slight,
Just actions sort trew from taint
Wake young warrior greet the morning light.

Ill fortune afflicts the dull and the bright,
Cities twinned, bridged with sacred paint;
Rise, rise: Carpe Diem yours by right.

Seeking moral balance twixt day and night,
Precious time, vernal equinox to sinner and saint
Wake young warrior greet the morning light.

Dies are cast as cords are sliced,
Genetic determined tho fate uncertain;
Rise, rise: Carpe Diem yours by right.

Life renews from ashed fright,
Use talents well, regret only wasted feint
Wake young warrior greet the morning light.
Rise, rise: Carpe Diem yours by right.

Sky Writer

Home, home on the range,

where deer and bobcat relay,

baton in motion.

Triggonometry

Liaisons bloom as you triangulate
caring not for whom you strangulate.
Stoically lip-serving the Old Man of Hoy
whilst brow-beating masses to cooperate.

Irony abounds in leaps of joy
promises found in the eyes of a boy.
Would he be kept in gilded cage
or swept to sea in ill-fated convoy.

History demands the turn of a page
destiny awaits in silent rage.
For Skefing set sail to craggy Orkney
as hearty a king known of the age.

Fortunes turned as Sirens did see
ship-wrecked survivor seed dynasty.
Fair-haired ruler planted tree
Stony ring for dowry.

Civic Discourse

Frontier dreams can hear;

Voices echoed from the past,

Ringin' talk of the town.

Bees of Promise

Eyes glimmer coat'd cocoa
abounded oases, peregrines pleasure.
Soaring o'er glorious plain'd-Pecos
alit upon verdant, terraced treasure.

Rivers o' milk and honey flow
o'er pitch-roofed golden flax.
Burgs abuzz with commerce grow;
rutting roads of well-combed wax.

Her dispatch twice-told to hatt'd judge
curried court of palm frond palace;
Aries horn gave gaveled cudgel
tempering just virgin chalice.

So far yon blaring horns of Jericho
chasing commissioned walls of woe.

Friendly Waters

Always of good humor
Jefferson's roads to be paved
Waltzin' Matilda.

Law of the Bone Yard

Sassafras lingered at Bean's Langtry
where whiskey held highest court;
The rope applied most liberally
as judge knew not writ from tort.

Solomon could not calm such fracas
where corpse commit calamity;
All the law west of the Pecos
would tend bar and sling irony.

Disputes were many tho' arguments few
rustlers, cardsharps, cheats and screws;
Knew justice was dispens'd by the pour
at regular intervals of ten, two, and four.

The Jersey Lily just by fate
barely missed a long waited date;
Tho olde Bean knew that'd somehow occur
'cuz he'd done earn'd his railroad spurs.

Image Manager

Dark focus astounds
Heart diamond shined most lovely
Apple o' her eye.

The Story of M

The universe expands,
the earth spins,
the faucet drips...

Mounds step into pyramids,
night moves into day,
the faucet drips...
noop, niiq, NOOP.

Volcanoes erupt,
glaciers melt,
the faucet drips...
niiq, noop, NIIQ.

Midnight nears,
thunder roars,
the faucet drips...
noop, niiq, NOOP.

Mountains thrust,
seas rise,
the faucet drips...
niiq, noop, NIIQ.

Edens spring from oases,
Moroccan paradise,
the faucet drips...
glib, glob, GLIB.

Rivers run thru us,
works reflecting dreams,
the faucet drips...

Singapore Sling

Eight parts gin to begin,
Add pineapple, cherry and cointreau;
Straight up on the rocks.

Parting Thoughts

Restless Winds

The words failed me,
at a loss to give voice
to wondrous cerebrations
racing through membranes,
packets forwarded,
bouncing off synapses,
gargling through ganglia,
rumbling the chords.
Sounds emerging,
disappointing in echo,
lacking in crispness,
monotonal fluff.
Resigned to muteness
I sat in silence
'til I heard
winds rustling trees.

Time After Time

Varangians in Virginia
Amazons in Arma
Jamestown to Jefferson
Kastrup to Karma

Richmond to Davis
John Smith to James Bond
Canute to Bognor
London to lama

Petticoats for Butterflies
Hollahs for Hammers
Deal for Powhatan
Oscar for Patton

History is More
than facts on a Page.
It's the flesh that explores
brings life to the age.

Waiting in the Wings

A wonderful life when measured by tray
to toil in shadows of pine mist.
Embraced by love in buffeted ways
hugged by jillions tho never kist.

Ironic twists abound in givers
in those who tend and mark time.
Exploring ponds, lakes and rivers
to their source poetic in rhyme.

Thru hurdles many and troubles colossal
the steady hand on keel carves a path
for those who can follow braided tassel
seeded bravely and jibed in math.

If in time you find a strawberry to spare
make sure and use it to colour the giant's hair

Aeolian Dreams

"What if the wind won't blow?"

A silent harp mocked the still'd mill blades,
as the flag went quiet and the beacon dim'd.

"Then the seed won't sow and the corn won't grow.
Hookers in the bay with sails long limp,
'll tug their moors 'long too calm shores,
stone walls keepin' the hunger entomb'd.
The bogs 'll get drained and the peat 'll rot high,
As the rye goes baid and the conne goe dry."

"Then why would you hope when to hope is conceit?"

Prodigal thorn guards bloom'd blush rose,
as wandering lamb hears its ewe's bold bleat.

"'Tis the way o' this land to breed stout plans,
so put it in your bag and keep a hale bonnet,
'cuz the wind's gonna blow and corn gonna grow,
whisky's gonna pour and the fish gonna jump.
The mill's gonna gin and the ship's 'll come in,
'n you'll be a hummin' your tune to an Aeolian dream.

Doors

The thing 'bout doors,
when it comes to the modes,
there must be a' least three....

The door that is open,
invites all to see,
Why pay-per-view?
It's all there for free.

The door that is shut,
breeds mistrust and contempt.
What have they to hide?
What makes them exempt?

Ah, but the door that's ajar,
now there's interest piqued.
There's more to discover,
for those that will seek.

A Note about the Author

Mark Bogdania was born in 1963 in Olathe, Kansas. He graduated from Kansas State University with bachelor's and masters' degrees in the Earth Sciences and was employed as a project manager with the U.S. Environmental Protection Agency prior to pursuing a PhD in Science Education at the University of Kansas. His first novel, *"The Amazing Double-Life of Marcus Pivo: Lviving with Agent Orange"* (2008) is a roman-a-clef work of fiction focusing on how a contamination release from one part of the planet could cause geopolitical mayhem in another portion of this ever shrinking world.

He developed a love for poetry while serving as an NSF Science Fellow in the Kansas City, Kansas Public School District where he used haiku writing as a form of learning assessment in the science classroom. While *Jump Joint & Other Scribbles* represents his debut book of poems, another composition, *Australia; Haiku'd Adventures in Oz* (2009) has also been sent for publication. This photo journal of the author's time spent "Waltzing Matilda" in the Land Down Under incorporates an original haiku with each image creating time capsulated vignettes.

Mark and his dog Snoopy live an amazingly normal life along the shores of Lake Michigan in Chicago, Illinois where he enjoys a well brewed beer while pondering all sorts of meta-physical things.

www.ingramcontent.com/pod-product-compliance
Lightning Source LLC
LaVergne TN
LVHW091206080426
835509LV00006B/854

* 9 7 8 0 6 1 5 3 2 5 7 9 8 *